Positive Affirmations For Women

250 Motivating Quotes & Affirmations

to Inspire your Wonderful Growth.

Emma Hyndall

©Copyright 2021 by Idyll Publishing

All rights reserved.

It is not legal to reproduce, duplicate, or transmit any part of this document in either electronic means or in printed format. Recording of this publication is strictly prohibited.

Prologue

Are you needing a little motivation? Or just wanting that little push? I want to welcome you to a new path, a new opportunity to grow. In the fore coming pages we are going to explore optimistic thoughts, and hack away at that negative thinking!

Excited?

A new approach is required to make change, so take a deep breathe, inhale positive energies, and exhale any negative thoughts. Make sure to take the time to really appreciate each thought. Visualize yourself conquering the day, completely focused, completely involved.

I wish you all the best and hope you can intimately fulfil your deepest longings.

Take a moment to be thankful for everything you've been through. You've prevailed. You came out strong. Congratulations beautiful.

Don't be afraid to start over again. This time you're not starting from scratch, you're starting from experience.

It's not hard. You've just never done it before. Know the difference. Engage your curiosity. Shift your perspective.

I am physically, mentally, and emotionally ready to enter a new phase in my life. I'm ready to grow and get better.

This year taught me that putting yourself first isn't selfish, it's necessary.

Concentrate on what you're doing. No distractions. Center yourself. This is your time.

You can be strong, confident, & independent and still be gentle, vulnerable & open.

You teach other people how to treat you by how you treat yourself.

Don't let the ugly in other people

kill the beauty in you.

A person that feels appreciated will always do

more than what is expected.

I pray you heal from all the things that no one

ever apologized for.

If you can't beat fear,

just do it scared.

Never tell people more than they need to know. Keep your life lowkey and let people assume incorrectly.

Drink water.

Eat healthy.

Meditate.

Mind your own business.

Create your visions.

Live your life.

Be the woman

you needed

as a girl.

Before I become the woman of your dreams,
I need to become the woman of my own
dreams first.

You get in life what you have the courage to
ask for.

The best thing I ever did was take
responsibility for my own success, happiness,
health, and peace.

I am strong. I am worthy.
I am beautiful. I am imperfect. I am me.

Honestly, the best thing you can do is to just try. Even if you're scared. Even if you don't know what the hell you're doing. Something good will come.

She wasn't looking

for a knight,

she was looking

for a sword.

Be careful with

who you share

your soul.

Goal:
To be so successful and independent that I can spoil myself, and do what I want daily.

Get your sh*t together, we're focusing on ourselves and our future from now on.

If you obey all the rules, you'll miss all the fun.

I have a great vision for my future & I now take steps forward towards my success.

Self-care isn't just drinking water and going to sleep early. Self-care is taking a break when things become overwhelming, saying no to things you don't want to do, allowing yourself to cry, asking for help from those around you, doing things that make you happy.

Staying positive doesn't mean you have to be happy all the time. It means that even on the hard days you know that there are better ones coming.

One day you will tell your story of how you've overcome what you went through and it will become part of someone else's survival guide.

The most convincing sign that someone is truly living their best life is their lack of desire to show the world that they're living their best life. Your best life won't seek validation.

Instead of worrying about what you cannot control, shift your energy towards what you can.

Gratitude helps you fall in love with the life you already have.

I want every girl to know that her voice can change the world.

It's okay if you thought you were over it but it hits you all over again. It's okay to fall apart even after you thought you had it under control. You are not weak. Healing is messy. There is no timeline for healing.

There's a difference between quitting and letting go, and it has to do with intention. You quit when you let your limiting beliefs get the best of you. You let go when something is no longer aligned.

Not everything that weighs

you down is yours to carry.

The best thing about life is that everything I've ever lost, has been replaced with something better. I never lack, I just transition.

Your life is in your hands. No matter where you are now, no what has happened in your life, you can begin to consciously choose your thoughts and you can change your life. There is no such thing as a hopeless situation. Every sing circumstance of your life can change.

Start:

Reading more.

Learning more.

Exercising more.

Being more.

You belong in this world just as much as anyone else. No matter how other see you, or how you see yourself.

Every morning you have to choices: Continue to sleep with your dreams or get up and chase them.

Train your mind to see the good in every situation.

Cross oceans for people. Love people, all people. No conditions attached, no wondering whether to not they're worthy. Cross oceans, climb mountains. Life and love isn't about what you gain, it's about what you give.

You are worthy.

I had to do a lot of healing, a lot of crying, a lot of sitting alone confused with myself to get here. But I really like this new version of myself.

Coffee in one hand, confidence in the other.

Life changes. You lose love. You lose friends. You lose pieces of yourself that you never imagined would be gone. And then, without even realizing it, these pieces come back. New love enters. Better friends come along. And a stronger, wiser you is staring back in the mirror.

I believe we need more leaders in this world who can use their gifts, talents and personal stories to serve others. There is someone out there who doesn't know you, who needs you in order to move to the next level in their life.

What right for her business, might not be right for yours. Stop comparing, start innovating.

I am gracefully letting go of what no longer serves me.

Dedicated, intelligent, and hard working. You are welcoming of new experiences, learning and growing into your true self.

Remember your goal.

Remember why you started.

Imagine the woman you want to be. What does she look like? Does she work for someone else? Or does she run her own show? What daily habits does she have? Start showing up as her every day. You don't become her like magic. You build her.

Best career advice that I can give: Don't ever attach yourself to a person, a place, a company, an organization or a project. Attach yourself to a mission, a calling, a purpose ONLY. That's how you keep your power and your peace.

Beware;

for I am fearless,

and therefore

powerful.

Stop letting your potential go to waste because you don't feel confident or ready enough. People with half your talent are making serious waves while you're still waiting to feel ready.

Create a to do list every day. Write down your goals, write down what you truly want from life. Manifest greatness, because you deserve the world.

I'm not afraid of failing.

I'm afraid of being in the same place I am now this time next year.

Find what works for you and double down on that. If that means quitting your job to build your business, do it. If that means spending less time with friends to get more work done, do it. Don't look back and regret not giving it your all.

Surround yourself with people that push you to do and be better. No drama or negativity. Just higher goals and higher motivation.

If you aren't willing to invest in yourself to get to that next level.

How can you expect to grow?

You are intelligent, capable, creative, and powerful. Now go out and get what's yours.

When you love yourself, you glow from the inside. You attract people who love, respect, and appreciate your energy. Everything starts with how you feel about yourself. Start feeling worthy, valuable and deserving of receiving the best that life has to offer. Be magnetic.

How to win in life:

Lift others up, even when you're at your lowest.

I owe it to myself to be consistent.
I owe it to myself to be disciplined.
I owe it to myself to stay focused.

When someone tells you that you're dreaming too big or to be more realistic, take that as a sign you're on to something great.

Never trade respect for attention.

When you ditch the excuses and stop with the limiting.

The only person you should ever compare yourself to is the person you used to be. Keep moving forward girl.

I dare you to dedicate the next 3 months exclusively to your goals. I don't think you will, prove me wrong.

You got to love the struggle just as much as the reward. So many people want the peak, but hate climbing. You want the success but don't want the struggle. See that's the problem… People want to grow, but don't want to go through the growing pains.

Stay away from everything that keeps you from your dreams.

Get honest with yourself. Look at your daily habits, thoughts, and actions. Ask yourself if your behavior is causing you to grow, decline, or stay stagnant. Are you going forward or going nowhere?

Sit with winners, the conversation will be different.

Make space for the next version of you… she's coming.

With every exhale, I release stress from my body.

Blocking people is a form of self-care.

Get around other women who talk about vision and ideas, not other people.

If you want a nice body, go get it. If you want to become a lawyer, study hard until you are one. If you want nice hair, pick a style and get it done. Stop being afraid and motivate yourself. Find your happiness, because it's out there waiting for you.

When you start noticing your worth, you will find it harder to stay around those who don't.

The real glow up is internal.

Self-reminder: you're still young and you're not supposed to have your whole life figured out yet. Don't stress. Everything will work out for the best

If you're going to try, go all in.

Deal with business, not with drama.

I wasn't ready for half the sh*t I went through, but clearly I was built for it.

She believed

she could

so she did.

Find someone who will take care of you. Not materialistically, but take care of your soul, your well-being, your heart, and everything that radiates within you.

Inner peace is the new success.

Get into the habit of asking yourself, "Does this support the life I'm trying to create?"

Even on the hardest of days, I'm still killing it.

I honor my need to rest and recharge. I am committed to finding ta least one hour of "me time" today.

Do yourself a favor and start believing that nothing is too good for you.

I am excited to show the world who I am and everything I have to offer. No one can stop me from meeting my goals.

I want to see what happens when I don't give up.

I'm in an uncomfortable stage of my life where my old self is gone but my new self isn't fully born yet. I'm in the midst of transformation.

Be your own kind of beautiful.

I enjoy being, feeling and thinking positive.

People set goals and the believe in them until their first failure. Success is built on a pile of failures. Build your commitment muscle.

Recognize when a phase, job, a life stage, or a relationship is over and let it go. Allow yourself to gracefully exit situations you have outgrown. Moving on doesn't have to be a catastrophic, dramatic event. You can simply choose to move forward with peace and clarity.

She's a queen,

with a little bit of savage.

If you hang out with me for too long, I'll brainwash you into believing in yourself and knowing you can achieve anything.

Repeat after me: My dream life, career, and income are possible. I have a plan and it's in motion. I'm going to make it happen no matter what.

Stop self-sabotaging yourself. Don't procrastinate. Don't be so critical. Forget your mistakes. You can do this, but only if you convince yourself you deserve great things.

There is nothing more sacred, more empowering, more beautiful, than very slowly becoming the woman I was destined to be.

Your perception of yourself affects your vibe. Love yourself, be confident in who you are, express your individuality and let your good vibes flow.

Opportunity is missed by most people because
it is dressed in overalls and looks like work.

When inner wisdom

speaks to you,

lean into that space

and listen.

You have to be disciplined. Discipline is doing
what you hate to do, but doing it like you love it.

I believe in myself and my abilities.
I am capable of anything I put my mind to.

Dear me, take a step back and breathe. Stop stressing and stop worrying. Get yourself together and do the things that you said you would do.

This is the mark of perfection; to spend each day as if it were your last, without frenzy, laziness, or any pretending.

Work while they sleep.

Learn while they party.

Save while they spend.

Live like they dream.

I finally realized I was not asking for too much, I was just asking the wrong person.

One day or day one.

You decide.

You're always one

decision off a completely

different life.

Note to self:

You have to do this for you. This is for you.
This isn't about anybody. Live for you. Honor
you. Never lose sight of that.

Life holds special magic

for those who dare to dream.

She came back a
completely different person.
She had changed.
The girl that cared what
everyone thought didn't
seem to care at all.
Her mind was clear.
She became free.

I am thankful, for my blessings are too
many to count.

I think when you're entirely honest with
yourself, a door opens within, and the light
unfolds, and everything painful flies away.

Do you want to meet

the love of your life?

Look in the mirror.

She slept with

wolves without fear,

for the wolves knew

a lion was among them.

Time for change,

time to restart,

time to conquer,

time to be fierce.

The time is now.

Learning how to leave people alone and move on with your life is a skill worth mastering.

You are braver then you believe, stronger than you seem, and smarter than you think.

Nobody gives you power.

You just take it.

Remember, comparison is the thief of joy.

Be mindful of what you accept as truth.
Because you become what you believe, for better or for worse.

Mood:

Listening and learning.

Growing and evolving.

Compassion and respect.

Open heart & open mind.

Speed doesn't matter,

progress is progress.

I am eternally grateful for my wonderful surroundings.

Protect your peace.

Get rid of toxicity.

Cleanse your space.

Cultivate love.

You're over here doubting yourself, while so many people are afraid of your potential.

Make friends who force

you to be better.

I never craved peace like I do now. I don't want to wake up bothered, angry, bitter, no negative energy or thoughts. I just want to be happy & at peace with everything.

You are glowing

just the way you are.

Don't let your loneliness make you reconnect with toxic people…

You shouldn't drink poison just because you're thirsty.

Life is so subtle sometimes that you barely notice yourself walking through the doors you once dreamed would open.

From little things,

big things grow.

My only goal in life right now is to be happy. Genuinely, intensely and consistently happy, regardless of what that looks like to others.

I never stop learning, and welcome any opportunity to grow.

You have as much time as you need.

Be the type of person who cheers on others, compliments strangers, and encourages people to believe in themselves. Kindness doesn't cost a thing.

Stop asking people who have never been where you're going for directions.

Appreciate the nuance of who you are. Find wonder in your surroundings. Notice the rainbows after the rain. And when rain gets you down, create your own sunshine because you are the only one who can.

A lot people are afraid to say what they want. That's why they don't get what they want.

I'm doing this for future me,

so that she gets to live the life that she deserves.

Remember:

It's possible to be a multifaceted woman. Read books & twerk. Be spiritual & a freak.

Spoke to my ex after 10 years.

"Miss or Mrs?" He asked.

Dr. I said.

3 things you should never feel guilty for: changing for the better, knowing your worth, staying true to your vision.

Creative energy surges through me and leads me to new and brilliant ideas.

A mistake that makes you humble holds greater value than an achievement that sours you with arrogance.

She overcame everything that was meant to destroy her.

Spend time in the company of those who can stand up for you when you are unable, those who believe in you when you are unwilling, those who honor the magnitude of your greatness, even when you are not quite ready to yourself.

Be the reason someone feels seen, heard, supported and valued.

Imagine where your life could be in 3 or 6 months from now once you decide to commit to yourself and your goals.

What a wonderful thought it is

that some of the best days of our

lives haven't happened yet.

You may not be there yet,

but you're closer than you

were yesterday.

Everything you want

is on the other side of consistency.

The question isn't who

is going to let me;

it's who is going to stop me.

She was focused

on self-growth,

business growth

and booty growth.

Define success on your own terms, achieve it
by your own rules, and build a life you're
proud to live.

Progress,

not

perfection.

Overthinking will destroy your happiness and your mood. It'll make everything worse than it actually is. Take a deep breath, exhale and have faith. What's meant to be will be.

Better an oops

than a what if.

At the end of the day I am an amazing woman. I'm not perfect by any means but my intentions are good, my heart is pure and I love hard with everything I have. I'm worth it. Always have been and always will be.

People are going to talk about you, no matter what you do. So you might as well do whatever brings you joy and live your best life.

The sun will rise

and we will try again.

I will forever remain humble because I know I could have less.

I will always be grateful because I know I've had less.

Don't compare your life to others. There's no comparison between the sun and the moon, they shine when it's their time.

You don't have to be anti-man to be pro-woman.

I attract the right people and the best circumstances for my highest good.

You don't always need a plan.
Sometimes, you just
need the courage.

Be loud about things
that are important to
you.

If it is not right, do not do it.

If it is not true, do not say it.

There's a message in the way a person treats you.

Just listen…

I'm not going to rush anything. I'm not going to stress out or worry about how things will work out for me. Instead of overthinking, I will align my faith with divine timing and trust that everything that belongs in my life is making its way towards me right now.

What's your favorite position?

CEO.

No matter what happens today, I know the truth that I am a radiant, powerful, and free woman.

Be humble, but aware of your value.

No success is too small to celebrate, and I revel in the tiny wins today.

Keep your heels, head, and standards high.

Goals so big you get uncomfortable telling small-minded people.

Don't put your happiness in other people's hands, they'll drop it. They'll drop it every single time.

Be the kind stranger someone remembers ten years from now.

Some acts of kindness are so needed, so touching, they're unforgettable.

Impossible is just an opinion.

Really think about your goals and how much energy you are truly putting into them. Your routine is costing you.

Growth looks so good on you. Keep doing you, babe.

Losing someone who doesn't appreciate you is a gain, not a loss.

When you admire something about another woman, tell her. Get in the habit of lifting each other up.

Difficult roads often lead to beautiful destinations.

By allowing myself to be happy, I inspire others around me to also feel happiness.

It's time to turn your energy all the way up to 11.

Stop explaining yourself to people who have proven they lack the mental capacity to understand you.

Your circle should want to see you win. Your circle should clap loudly when you have good news. If not, you need a new circle.

While you're working for what you want, don't forget to be grateful for what you already have.

Do it because your kids deserve a mother they can brag about.

There is peaceful.

There is wild.

I am both at the same time.

When you're confident in what you bring to the table, you don't have to beg anyone to sit down and eat.

Let go of everything you didn't do right, the negative things people have said, and focus on all you are becoming.

"What if I fall?"

Oh, but my darling…

What if you fly?

Repeat daily:

I am in charge of how I feel, and today I am choosing happiness.

She has been through hell. So believe me when I say, fear her when looks into a fire and smiles.

The biggest lie we are told is "Be with someone who makes you happy." The truth is, happiness is something you create on your own. Be with somebody that adds to it.

More focused on where I'm going than who's not coming.

Have you ever been so disappointed by someone that you forgive them and don't say anything, but in your head you detach yourself from them completely?

Some women

fear the fire.

Some women

become it.

Look at you go, you're so tired but are not giving up! I'm so proud of you.

It's okay to unfollow people in real life.

Don't worry about how many mistakes you'll make or how slow you're progressing. You're still a million miles ahead of those not starting.

Be the woman who fixes another woman's crown without telling the world it was crooked.

Investing in women means investing in the people who invest in everyone else.

One thing my mother taught me was RESPECT. I greet the janitor with the same level of respect I greet the CEO.

Privacy is power. What people don't know they can't ruin.

One small positive thought in the morning can change your whole day.

Life is so much simpler when you stop explaining yourself to people and just do what works for you.

You're literally doing you best and if no one is proud of you, be proud of yourself.

You'll be amazed at what you'll attract when you start believing in what you deserve.

There is nothing stronger than a broken women who has rebuilt herself.

She's badass with a good heart, soft but strong. Unapologetic and honest. She's the type of women you go to war beside, the type of woman you marry.

Here's to strong women,

may we know them,

may we be them,

may we raise them.

Above all,

be the heroine of your life,

not the victim.

There's nothing more powerful than a woman who chooses to believe in herself and goes all in on her dreams.

Journal Space

Please use this space below to journal your goals, write down your strengths and weaknesses, compile your favorite quotes and affirmations, or anything you wish. I encourage you to self-reflect and journal these conversations with yourself as a healthy outlet and a measure of accountability.

_____

_____

_____

_____

_____

_____

_____

_____

Epilogue

Well, here we are. Congratulations on your effort! How do you feel? Uplifted I hope! Brimming with confidence, inspired to face anything thrown in your direction.

Please refer back to this book any time you need motivation, or any words of inspiration. I recommend you surround yourself with other like-minded, positive and successful people and watch as you lift each other up beyond expectation. Know that we are all in this together and want nothing more than to help each other level up.

Lastly, I send nothing but love and encouragement your way. I truly believe you will find your motivation and achieve everything you desire. Keep smiling girl, you got this.

If you enjoyed this book, it would be sincerely appreciated if you could leave a review on Amazon. I would love to read your story, and how you are progressing towards a better version of yourself.

-Emma Hyndall

www.ingramcontent.com/pod-product-compliance
Lightning Source LLC
Chambersburg PA
CBHW071756080526
44588CB00013B/2264